W9-CUA-100

Surfing:
How to Improve
Your Technique

Surfing:
How to Improve
Your Technique

by Mark Sufrin

FRANKLIN WATTS, INC. • NEW YORK
1973

Illustrations by Orin C. Kincade
Cover by Michael Horen

Photograph Credits
Jack Zehrt, vi, 57/ Dick McCoullough, Alpha Photo Asso-
ciates, Inc., 4/ Florida News Bureau, 13/ Herb Nose-
worthy, 14/ Photoworld, Inc., 17/ Ed Greevy, 19, 35, 48/
Richard Stelhorn, 23/ John H. Atkinson, Jr., 26, 32, 54,
58/ Bruce Davidson, Magnum Photos, 28/ Leroy F. Gran-
nis, Globe Photos, 37, 50/ Werner Stoy, Camera Hawaii,
38/ United Press International, 47/ John R. Hamilton,
Globe Photos, 55.

Library of Congress Cataloging in Publication Data
Sufrin, Mark.
    Surfing: how to improve your technique.

    (A Concise guide)
    SUMMARY: Describes the basic equipment and
fundamental techniques of surfing including safety tips
and a glossary of terms.
    Bibliography: p.
    1. Surf riding–Juvenile literature. [1. Surf riding]
I. Title.
GV840.S8S73   797.1'72   73-2942
ISBN 0-531-02628-0

Contents

A glorious ride

Introduction

The sport of surfing began early in man's history in the islands of the Western Pacific. The people who first learned to capture the energy of the surf and use it for their pleasure were Polynesians, who probably lived on Tahiti and Bora Bora.

A group of Polynesians left their home islands sometime between A.D. 800 and 1100 and migrated eastward to Hawaii. In 1778, Captain James Cook, the English explorer, took his ship into Hawaii. Cook and his astonished crew spotted some men who appeared to be flying over the water. What they saw were Hawaiian nobles riding the waves on their huge wiliwili wood boards — *the first surfers.*

Today surfing is popular wherever there is great ocean water to challenge the surfer. Nobody can "outfight" the sea by sheer strength, but the surfboard is man's "tool" to overcome its power. Anyone who enters and rides the sea does it by skill, not with brute strength.

Surfing is one of the most exciting sports in the world, and one of the most unique. It has its own drama, fascination, thrills, chills, and spills. The beginning surfer will meet all of these as he learns and progresses. No one can tell the novice in advance what he will find — or how he will react to it. Surfing is not only one of the most exciting and graceful of sports — it is also one of the most unpredictable.

No two waves are ever alike, and no two surf rides are ever the same. Surfing is a challenge to the mind and body. You have entered another element — the pounding, shifting, ever-changing sea. The sea can never be mastered. You must always respect it as an antagonist, but, as a surfer, you can learn to live in it, ride on it, and experience thrills you'll never forget.

In surfing you meet the challenge alone. There are no team-

1

mates to help you or to cover up your mistakes. It takes hard work and long hours to train your body and learn the necessary skills. Surfing is much more than a plunge into the sea with a board and then the long, skimming ride back to shore. To be a good surfer you must have dedication, courage, and imagination.

But the rewards in surfing are great. Surfing teaches you to overcome the hazards of a great natural force and — for short, exciting bursts — to become one with it. Surfing gives you confidence, involves all your senses, and gives you a feeling of freedom and accomplishment that is unequaled in any other sport.

For the beginner learning in gentle surf, the goal and dream of every surfer looms ahead — big-wave surfing — somehow managing to ride in safety on a sliver of board along challenging waves that have the power to toss a locomotive like a toy.

But all that lies in the future. . .

Now let's get down to basics.

Getting Started

Health

Surfing is a strenuous sport that places great demands on the muscles, the heart, and the respiratory system. It doesn't demand brute strength, but like every sport, surfing requires a well-conditioned body and good health (although people with handicaps can learn to surf).

You're fortunate to begin surfing early. Young people are more supple and respond to training quickly. Their muscles and body tone develop rapidly to meet the demands of swimming and paddling that are so necessary to the sport.

The single most important need for surfing is the body's ability to recover normally from fatigue. Every time you launch your board, paddle out, and return to shore, your arms and back and lungs get a terrific workout. And when you spill, as you are likely to do as a beginner, you will expend great energy fighting the water.

You should get yourself into the best possible physical shape. Eat sensibly, get plenty of sleep, and don't train haphazardly. There is no magic formula for becoming a good surfer, but you'll give yourself the best start possible if you're in good shape. It might mean giving up some of the things you like. Instead of cakes and candy and sodas and potato chips, you should eat foods that are high in energy and protein, which build muscle. Instead of staying up late to watch television, get the amount of sleep needed for good health, and instead of horsing around with your friends in some aimless game, go to an indoor pool and develop your swimming muscles. You'll need these muscles in surfing. Remember, you don't need a gym or complicated equipment to get into good physical condition.

3

A beginner's spill

A Basic Skill

The one skill that is absolutely necessary for surfing is swimming, since everything else in the sport is based on this. *Don't try to become a surfer unless you can swim.* You don't have to be a fast swimmer, but you must have very good stamina, a fair amount of power, and what might be called "savvy" — knowing what you're doing at all times in the water.

This book is intended as a basic guide to surfing, but you can't learn how to swim or surf by reading books or magazines. At best these can be a guide, to give you some idea of what to do. But actual experience is absolutely necessary. If you have an instructor — an older brother or sister, your father, the older surfers at the beach, or someone trained to teach surfing — so much the better.

To participate in any sport you must begin with a strong, healthy body. But modern coaches tell us that athletes must train differently for different sports. Running, for instance, will greatly benefit the basketball, football, or tennis player, by building up his legs and wind. Running, however, can only help a surfer develop good body tone. The strengths necessary to surfing — strong shoulder, back, and arm muscles — can't be developed by running. There are, however, many exercises you can do out of the water that will develop the power you'll need.

Don't forget: *a surfer is challenging one of the great forces of nature!* Surfing can be a dangerous sport and every precaution should be taken to ensure safety. The only way you'll *know* you're safe in the water is if you can swim well. *A surfer who can't swim is like a skydiver without a parachute.* You should learn to swim underwater as well as on the surface and be able to tread water for long periods.

The surfer — even the young beginner — should have the physical strength to keep control of his board while paddling

5

outward through the waves. Before you ever enter the ocean to try surfing, you should develop the necessary skills in a swimming pool or lake if possible. You can do many exercises to develop your shoulders, back, and arms. (Don't think it's quicker if you use weight-training.) Developing a good kick is a little more specialized. One very valuable exercise for doing this is to use a small float or kickboard and propel yourself only by using your legs in the breaststroke (frog), scissors, or flutter kick.

Being a strong swimmer means that you can swim a good distance and still be able to climb out on shore and stand up without breathing heavily. Even low surf can create dangerous currents and churning, turbulent water. A surfer who loses his board after a wipe-out may be taken a long distance from shore by a rip current. If you can't stay afloat for a long time and swim a good distance, you're in trouble. Surfing on a lake along the wake of a powerboat is safer because the water is calm and help is near at hand. This kind of surfing, by the way, is excellent training for the ocean.

Learn to use your strength and energy in the best possible way. If you find yourself getting tense, and your body is becoming all knotted up, you are getting a warning — *you're trying too much too fast.* You need to be stronger, to get more confidence, and to have greater knowledge of the situation. It's fine for a football player to be "in there fighting." For a surfer it's bad. It means you're just wasting energy. You aren't beating the surf — you're beating yourself. A gymnast, weight-lifter, high-jumper, or pole-vaulter often has to make a supreme effort in a single instant. But the surfer should never have to feel that at any moment he has to give his all.

6

Body Surfing

Body surfing is a good way to become familiar with the ways of the surf. Sliding waves with the body instead of a board can be enjoyed at most ocean beaches. Body surfing is perhaps the purest form of wave riding. Nothing separates you and the wave. Body surfing has been called "the best possible type of training for board-surfing, a skill splendidly suited to build better all-around surfers."

Best of all, body surfing can be done at many public beaches where surfing with a board is prohibited. Waves of three feet and up breaking at least ten yards from shore are necessary for body surfing. The only type of wave that can't be ridden is the crashing beach-pounder that curls and dumps in shallow water or a wave that breaks in deep water without a steep face to slide on.

The principles behind catching a wave with the body are just about the same as for board riding. The swimmer places himself in a spot just shoreward of where the wave will begin to break. If you are too far inshore when the wave breaks, the forward slope of the wave will be destroyed, making it impossible to ride. If you try to pick up the wave too soon, the face of the wave won't be steep enough to let your body slide. The big difference between board and body surfers is that the body surfer usually rides in the white water whereas the board rider tries to avoid it.

Beginners often ask about the use of fins in body surfing. Possibly they've used them in a pool or lake, or in calm water while swimming in the ocean. There is one definite rule about fins that all surfers should obey: *A swimmer should never use fins to get himself into any surf situation that he'd avoid without them.* Fins can be a valuable aid to swimmers, but fins are too often used as a substitute for swimming skill — and because of that they can be dangerous.

Remember, if you swim well, all the other skills of surfing

7

can be developed. Without these other skills, progress in surfing is either impossible or foolhardy.

The United States Surfing Association believes that a beginner should be able to swim a short distance at top speed, a longer distance at a slower, steady pace, remain underwater for at least twenty seconds, and have the physical strength to control his surfboard while paddling outward through at least two sets of breaking waves.

At the Beach

Take It Easy and Slow

When you are on a beach where a good surf is running, it is advisable to take things easy for a while. *Never leap into the surf immediately! And never take a dare from anyone!* There are always clowns who think they know it all, or can do it the easy way, or want to be like the "big guys." Remember that to be a good surfer you have to know the sea and wind and currents, as well as your board. Don't take chances. Don't overreach yourself. Never forget that you are a land animal, *and every moment you're in the sea you're in a hostile place.*

Make friends with the sea. Watch the waves for a time, notice the patterns in which they break, how often they break, whether they break from right to left or the reverse, and how fast they come into shore. Take note of the direction of the wind, for it can become an important factor in producing big exciting waves, and also a threat when it whips the sea into rough, raging water.

Stroll along the waterline and wade out slowly to your knees. In other words, get acquainted with the sea, know its tug and pull, learn the way the waves feel when they break over you, get wet all over, and experience the buoyancy of seawater. Your body will begin to make small adjustments to the water, and even fairly strong waves will begin to seem easier as you learn to live in another element.

Your Board

Almost anything can be used to practice paddling and kicking. Some beginners use an air mattress because it is highly buoyant and compact. An air mattress is also good because it can be used in deeper water and is relatively safe. You can also use a "belly board," which is really just a short surfboard.

Both the mattress and belly board serve their purpose, but to really learn how to surf it is best to start with a standard-sized board. Any reputable sporting goods store will sell you the correct board. You should be careful if you are buying a used board. It will cost only a few dollars less and often may be cracked and parched, although the damage and repairs are barely visible. Here are some guidelines on board sizes:

• If you weigh under 100 pounds, your board should be 8 feet 9 inches long, 21-1/2 inches wide, and 2-3/4 inches thick.

• If you weigh between 100 and 120 pounds, your board should be 9 feet long, 22 inches wide, and 3 inches thick.,

• If you weigh between 120 and 150 pounds, your board should be 9-1/2 feet long, 22 inches wide, and 3 inches thick.

• If you weigh between 150 and 175 pounds, your board should be 9-3/4 feet long, 23 inches wide, and 3-1/2 inches thick.

• If you weigh between 175 and 200 pounds, your board should be 10 feet long, 23-1/2 inches wide, and 4 inches thick.

These dimensions are all on the slightly oversized and buoyant side. A buoyant board is called a *floater* and is easier to handle. It paddles better and catches waves quicker. A board that is too small for the surfer's weight tends to sink and is hard to paddle. If the board is too big, it will paddle well but it is difficult to turn and control in a wave. If the board is too wide, it will rub against the inside of the arms, which makes it difficult to dig in and take a full stroke when paddling.

Undertows rip tide

Before we get down to surfing itself, we should consider one other hazard of the sport. You are probably aware of the myth

10

of a dreadful sea monster called "The Undertow" that waits to seize unwary swimmers and surfers. Undertows are believed to be strong currents that flow seaward along the bottom, below the incoming breakers, at speeds greater than the average swimmer can combat. The simple truth is that there is no such thing. Undertows don't exist any more than do mermaids or Davy Jones's locker. The belief in an undertow is as much superstition as is the notion that every ninth wave — or seventh — or third — will be bigger than the rest.

The sea presents enough dangers and problems without your being afraid of the undertow. Like many myths, this one has a small basis in fact. Sometimes, especially on beaches with steep slopes, there are powerful runbacks or backwashes of water. Such a backwash may easily pull a wader's feet out from under him. Scrambling to his feet, the confused, frightened person might then be knocked down by an incoming wave. As a beginning surfer, you should be wary of backwashes, but you also should not panic at the thought of nonexistent undertows.

Surfing
Fundamentals

A great deal can be learned by watching other surfers and the action of the breaking waves. But just watching doesn't help you develop balance or learn the fine points of surfing.

The beginner should practice the basic techniques of paddling and board control before trying to catch the first wave. Without a good background of paddling, catching that first wave may become so difficult it might discourage you before you really get started.

It takes a certain amount of skill and strength to paddle a board out through a set of breakers, spin it around, and paddle again to catch a ride. Paddling is the best way to train for surfing, and paddling skillfully is half the battle of learning how to surf.

A good paddler gets the most out of his board with the least expense of energy. When you paddle well, you move through the water faster, pick up a wave with only a few strokes, and feel in balance whether you are standing or paddling. Good board handling also adds to the safety of surfing. If a surfer caught in a set of big waves can paddle well, he can avoid being washed back or wiped out. If not — the waves win and he will face a long swim back to shore.

Handling the Surfboard

Boards are awkward to carry, by hand or car. A board dropped on rock or pavement will usually break. If you drop a board on your toes or foot, you'll limp the rest of the day. Carrying a board at a crowded beach can cause problems. If the board is

Carrying boards

carried at its center of balance and is always pointed ahead, the tail won't swing sideways. Surfboards should be carried under the arm, with the hand and fingers curled around the bottom rail. If your arm is too short for this method, carry the board with the lower edge resting in the crook of your arm and the upper edge resting against the shoulder. Boards can also be carried on the head. A small towel between your head and the board can make this a comfortable position.

Remember that you have a jutting skeg (fin) at the tail; always keep it pointed toward you. If the path to the beach is steep and rocky, wear sneakers. They'll prevent bruised feet and a dropped board. If you carry the board on top of a car, make sure it is tightly fastened to the roof rack.

Waxing

Waxing

A board can be waxed at any time, but it is quite pleasant to do this on the beach under a warm sun that helps melt and spread the wax. Slipping is one of the major problems in paddling or riding a board. The smooth fiberglass covering becomes very slippery when wet. This helps on the bottom of the board, but on the top, where you are, it can lead to fast wipe-outs and the loss of the board in the surf. You can choose from many varieties of wax at any surfing equipment store. But you don't have to be fussy, almost any wax will do.

Many surfers carry a small piece of wax in their trunks and wax their boards while waiting for a wave. If your supply of wax is short, wax the bottoms of your feet rather than only a small portion of the board.

Be careful of suntan oil. A few drops on a board can invite disaster. It makes the board as slippery as butter in a skillet.

Don't overdo the waxing. Skiers make a ritual of it because they have to adjust to different kinds of snow conditions. You are only seeking good friction.

Launching the Board

Check the shoreline for the following:

Is the bottom rocky or sandy?

Is there a drop into deep water?

Is there marine life — sea urchins, crabs, mussels, and the like — to cut and bruise your feet?

Will breaking waves wash the board back?

A sandy bottom is no problem. It is difficult, however, to wade out over rocks when slightly off balance because you're carrying a board. Along a rocky shore beach, look for channels through which you can enter deeper water and start paddling. If the surf is rolling into shore and you must fight through the waves, wait for a calm period and then go — quickly! Waves usually come in sets, and a few minutes wait for a calm will spare you trouble. If you have to wade out over rocks, turn the board upside down. This places the skeg in the air and keeps it from snagging on the way out. Some lightweights who float high on their boards can paddle out over the rocks with their boards upside down.

When walking out through small breaking surf, hold the board high and let the waves pass under it. Keep the nose of the board up. If it is pointed down, a wave will tear it from your grip. Always keep the board pointed straight ahead. If it is turned sideways when a wave hits, the board will *broach* (turn sideways and over) and will be pulled away or washed into you. Being

15

Standard position for knee paddling

struck by a loose board is no fun. If your board is pointed into the surf, it will probably punch through the wave and come through in good shape.

Paddling

The two main paddling positions are the *prone* and *kneeling*. If you have done the preliminary paddling practice as recommended, the prone position will seem familiar to you. Prolonged fast paddling even on an easy moving board isn't simple. Your first practice spins should be done in calm waters near shore, on days with little wind. Expert surfing instructors all recommend that beginners take things gradually as they build up their paddling power.

The secret of paddling well lies in good balance and in using your muscles properly. Try to find your board's center of balance quickly — and keep the weight of your body as far as possible over the center line. Your weight should also be placed so that the nose of the board is just an inch or two above the level of the water. If the nose is too low, it will scoop up water and dig in. If it is too high, the tail will drag, create resistance, and you'll have trouble paddling.

Paddling — prone and sitting

When the water is choppy, keep the nose slightly higher than usual so that the water won't wash over it. If your body goes sideways, the board leans and will tip with the slightest wave or slap of rough water. Hold your head high and keep a sharp lookout for waves — and other boards or any floating obstacles. Paddling out in good-sized surf is a bit like running across a busy highway. But if you know what's coming at you at all times and don't get flustered, you can move ahead, go sideways, or retreat.

Prone Paddling

This is the easiest position to learn because the center of balance is low and there is less danger of tipping. The chin-up position should be held for prone paddling because it helps arch the back

17

so that more muscles are brought into play when you stroke. The arms, shoulders, and back work together, and their combined power can really make your board go surprisingly fast and far.

Always keep in mind that your body is arched and your weight is carried on the lower chest, stomach, and thighs. When you make your first attempts at prone paddling, keep your legs together, with your knees as close together as comfort allows. After you've gained confidence, you can do what many surfers do — paddle with one leg bent at the knee and the foot sticking up in the air. This seems to be a natural body reaction that helps you keep balance. The foot moves from side to side in the opposite direction of a tip, tending to keep the board level.

The paddling stroke is a natural overarm throw combined with dipping the hands and arms into the water and pulling back and through. Keep your fingers relaxed to reduce tension and fatigue. Paddling is a *pull — recover — rest — pull* cycle. The board glides ahead when the arms come out of the water. The recovery is relaxed, giving the muscles time to rest. When you gain confidence in your paddling, you can get more speed by *feathering* your hands after each stroke; that is, turning your hands parallel to the rails of the board to reduce drag.

Knee Paddling

Once you become comfortable paddling prone, try the knee position. This requires a little more balance, but it is really easy. Many young surfers seem to paddle only on their knees; they think it gives them a faster start than the prone position. Also, while paddling prone a surfer may feel a lot of pressure on the bottom of his rib cage, and getting on his knees will relieve the pain.

Sit back on your heels between strokes. When you paddle, the body rocks forward and the weight shifts forward from the

18

Knee paddling

center of balance. The hands dig in and the body rocks back. Both the muscles and the movement of your body rocking back add to the force of the stroke in knee paddling. For power and stamina, nothing beats the kneeling position. One other advantage of kneeling on the takeoff is the quickness with which your center of balance can be shifted when you're digging to catch a wave.

When paddling down the wave on a takeoff, it is sometimes necessary to move your balance point forward or backward. Moving the balance point *forward* increases the downward tilt of the board and helps speed the slide down the wave. Moving the weight *back* reduces the slide angle and sometimes prevents a *pearl* (when the nose drops enough to dig in and slow or stop the board). When a board pearls, a rider usually falls.

19

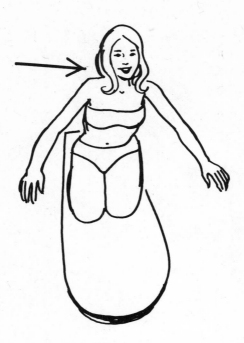

Turning by leaning toward the direction to be turned

Paddling can also be done while sitting with the feet on the board. It is comfortable, casual, not very powerful, and is used mainly for moving short distances while keeping in position for a wave.

Some surfers paddle only with their legs. This is not very effective, just something to fool around with if the wait between sets of waves is very long. You simply do a bicycling motion of the legs in the water.

Turning the Board

Turning the board is an important skill in paddling. Slight, slow turns are done by leaning toward the direction in which you

Turning by dragging one foot

want to turn. Some surfers drag a foot to help turn the board, using the foot as a rudder. Dragging the right foot while paddling will turn the board to the right. A complete about-face is made by sitting at the tail end of the board and raising about two-thirds of the board out of the water. The nose of the board can then pivot around the tail. Both the arms and legs help turn the board around in a pivot turn. To turn right both legs rotate counterclockwise; to turn left both rotate clockwise.

Many surfers face out to sea while waiting for a wave — and then spin around quickly as the wave comes. At the end of the turn they throw their weight forward and start to paddle. This sudden shift of weight forward seems to accelerate the start and they catch the wave in fewer strokes.

A surfer once said: "Paddling is the price you pay to reach a position where you can catch the wave." The better and

A complete about-face

stronger and more versatile paddler you are, the more complete
surfer you'll be.

Paddling Out

Perhaps one day there will be a helicopter service to transport
surfers and their boards beyond the breakers — like an aerial
"surf lift" resembling today's ski tows. But until that time it is
still the surfer against the sea as he goes out to catch a wave.

Watch the surf before going out. On some days waves come
into shore in a definite pattern or set. There is no reason for you
to waste energy fighting through a broken surf when in a few
minutes the sets of waves will get smaller and a calm period will
follow.

Spot the best place to catch a wave, keep an eye out for all

Paddling out

possible hazards, and judge the best way of going out. On some days, after a storm, for example, waves roll in continuously with no period of calm, or lull, between sets. On such days, try to find a channel of calmer water to paddle out through. At most surfing beaches it is also possible to paddle around the break of the waves. Getting around the end takes less fight, reduces the

23

chance of another board hitting you, and is often quicker than a direct route out.

As a beginner you'll probably be in surf with generally small and weak waves. While prone, simply paddle toward the wave hard and fast and, at the instant of contact, turn your face to avoid the full impact of the white water. If you're kneeling, push hard directly at the wave and raise your body from the waist until your trunk is upright at the moment of contact. The kneeling paddler can often raise himself up on two feet, as if about to stand. You are, in effect, standing for just that brief moment during which your board meets and passes through white water.

Sometimes, when prone, you will see that you can push your way through a wave but know that you're going to get a face full of white water. To avoid this, wait until the moment of contact, grab the rails of the board about on a level with your shoulders, and push up (as if you were doing a regular push-up in a gym). This allows the foam that comes over the nose of the board to flow harmlessly between your body and the board.

If you are ever caught suddenly by a big wave that is too much for you to handle, there is an exciting and safe way to escape it. You *turn turtle*. This means flipping the board over you and hanging on while the board passes overhead. If it is big surf, wrap your legs and arms around the board. The body hanging onto the board acts as a sea anchor and prevents it from being washed back too far. Having the board overhead also protects you from other boards coming down at you from every angle.

The First Rides

Remember — until you have gained skill and confidence, your first rides should be in the prone position — and the best beginning is to catch a wave that is already broken.

Paddle your board to a zone where incoming *broken waves* are running in a moderate height — from two to three feet. Turn your board so that it is parallel to the shoreline, and watch the incoming surf to right and left. When an incoming swell is approaching, you begin to turn the nose of your board toward shore. You start to dig in, hard and strong. Even as the broken wave draws near, your board is already going at a good rate. You continue to gain speed — it's as if you're trying to escape the wave. But if your timing is right, the wave will always catch you.

The moment of contact! In a split second you feel the thrilling sensation of the wave "taking hold" and carrying your board. Paddling halts just after the take-hold is completed. Your board is now "in" the broken wave. If you keep your board properly balanced, you can ride the wave all the way into shore. But always try to finish a ride well before your fin begins to drag in bottom sand or scrapes against the rocks.

A lot of changes can happen during such a ride on a broken wave. The foam of a large broken wave may cover you completely for a time and then seem to pass you by. This "lost-in-the-white water" sensation might continue for a few seconds in a big broken wave. But if the surfer keeps good momentum and balance, his board will be pushed out ahead of the wave before long.

For at least your first twenty rides or so, you should start and finish a ride in the prone position — even if it seems a bit tame after a while. As your board rides with the wave, you can

25

keep experimenting: a little extra paddling; counterpaddling; hand-braking; adjusting trim, tilt, and balance. You can learn a great deal that is valuable in those first rides. Prone-surfing isn't just a good introduction to surfing: it is an absolutely necessary part of the complete surfer's skills.

From Prone to Kneeling

When you've grown used to riding prone, you can move to a kneeling position during a ride by this easy method: without releasing your grip on the board rails, pull your knees forward one at a time until you are in the knee-paddling stance described earlier. Then begin to release your grip on the rails and use your arms to help balance the board.

Successful rides in the kneeling position will encourage you to a further step: riding on small broken waves by knee-paddling rather than doing it prone. This requires great skill in balancing because the body's center of gravity is now high above the board. From time to time you may have to place a hand on the deck to steady yourself and the board. But continued practice will soon have you keeping the no-hands position — and then going beyond that.

You can now start from broken waves caught a little farther out and sooner after their first breaking. As these rides continue, you are almost sure to discover one important thing — your ride, although it seems "welded" to the wave, does allow for some angling or turning. This turning is first noticed when, accidentally or otherwise, the board is tilted to the right or left as it moves.

Now you begin to use intentionally what you may have noticed happened only by accident. You begin to work on your

White water

27

Ready and waiting to catch a wave

turns. By forcing down the left side of the board while raising the right, a turn is made toward the left. This is the familiar leaning turn known to anyone who rides a bicycle or a skate board, and to every skier.

Catching the Wave

At this stage you should be a good swimmer, a strong paddler, and have experience riding the broken wave. It is time to graduate to another basic surfing skill. You can begin to catch waves that have not yet broken, but staying in the prone position.

Suppose you have a day when the surf isn't high. The waves

28

Riding in a kneeling position

are coming in regular sets so that you can time them more easily. You have paddled out to a spot close enough to the breaking waves to catch one.

The waiting game begins. In surfing it is always hurry out and wait for a wave. Most days the wait will be just long enough to rest tired muscles. But you're lucky. A set is coming in and you start to judge in your mind the best place to be when your wave arrives. You turn your board shoreward and get set. You're alone now and your stomach is probably tense with excitement. The wave comes swiftly — and now is the time to paddle. You start. The wave is directly behind you, and your board is at right angles to it. You glance over your shoulder to see what the wave is doing. You see white water starting off to your left, but far enough away so that you know it won't spill over you. Even if the wave begins to collapse, there is a way to pull out — you can stop the board quickly by sliding back toward the tail.

But everything looks *Go!* You dig in with one final strong pull. The swell comes, the nose of the board tips down, the tail rises, and you begin to slide. This is the thrill of the start . . . the slide . . . the sense of motion that says you're starting your ride and the energy of the sea and surf has caught you. It is at this precise moment, when you feel that you're in harmony with a great natural force, that you experience the thrill of surfing — you're in a wave and your board is sliding by wave force alone.

It's like flying. Now it seems terribly steep. White water breaks over the back of the board, spray is hitting in your eyes as you hang on and get a slightly bouncy ride all the way into shore.

Perhaps, on repeated rides, you aren't exactly a graceful sea creature. But you've learned some valuable lessons: you notice that the slight shift of balance on the takeoff might mean catching the wave or not. Too far forward on the board causes pearling; too far back causes you to stall. You also learn to recover from a possible wipe-out by turning back into a wave and shifting your weight to the back of the board.

But the most important thing you learn on these first prone rides is the exciting feeling of the takeoff and slide. You now know what to expect the next time so that you can pay greater attention to form and style.

Many basic skills can be learned riding prone or kneeling. Don't feel self-conscious surfing this way at first. Other more experienced surfers, who look so great now, went through the same learning experience. Having caught the first waves prone or kneeling, you can then try turning quicker, taking off closer to the breaking portion of the wave, and seeing how changes in balance affect the board. If your board gets too low in the water, it will be harder to control. Riding the wave near the top permits a faster pullout if the wave begins to collapse.

Don't try too much the first day. You'll grow tired and sometimes confused. This is usually because of inexperience and lack of good physical condition. It is best to take a short rest after paddling out. While the arms rest and the breath returns, you can get into position for the next wave. *If you feel tired — head back to the beach immediately!* Cold and fatigue mean wasted effort, missed waves, and wipe-outs. Most important — you don't have the strength to fight the power of the sea.

Standing

Every beginning surfer should find out for himself — before ever going into the water — whether he's naturally a right- or left-foot-forward-rider. The test is simple. Run a short distance and then slide on a smooth surface. Which foot is in front? If it's your right foot, it's almost certainly better for you to do your surfing that way. If it's your left foot, then your body makeup and habits make a left-foot-first surfer. Most surfers seem to do it that way. But it doesn't really matter. Whichever is comfortable for you. Many surfers can switch to either foot and it doesn't hurt their performance.

It is best to practice your first moves from prone to kneeling to standing in calm water. Standing up on the board can be done at any time during the first part of the ride. Experienced surfers usually get to their feet quickly, turn the board at the right moment, and slide away on a wave. The beginner should wait until the board is turned and riding smoothly before standing. Many beginners jump to their feet too soon, causing the board to stall out or nose down and pearl. Trying to catch a wave that's too small or one without enough slope is also a waste of energy.

Rising to a standing position

To stand, either come directly to your feet in one smooth motion or rise to the knees in a crouch and then stand up. The back leg sends changes of body balance to the board. The farther back the weight is placed and the greater the lean toward the face of the wave, the faster the board will turn. A sharp movement of this kind will produce the pullout. Moving the weight forward toward the nose will drop it until it digs in and pearls. This is another type of pullout. A carefully balanced

32

Basic stand-up position

forward position will result in the best speed, but is difficult to hold.

In the basic stand-up position the feet are usually spread about eighteen inches apart (a little more or less according to how tall you are and what feels comfortable), and the rear foot is turned at almost right angles to the center line of the board. The body can face directly forward or be turned about forty-five degrees off the center line (an imaginary line running down the middle of the board from nose to tail). The standing position will vary with the individual surfer and the kind of waves and the general surf and wind conditions. Practice will help determine what's best for you.

Every new ride adds to your surfing education. You'll learn many things for yourself that can be described in a book but that have real meaning for you only when you experience them. You'll find, for instance, that the suggested ways to place the feet are just points to start from. You aren't fixed to the board in any one place or position. Your freedom to shift is necessary both for balance and for control in turning, stalling, and so on.

On your first rides you'll experiment, discovering how every move you make on the board leads to changes in the way it behaves and in the relation of your body to the board. Some changes will give you what you want and others will bring about effects you don't want or expect. Bit by bit, you'll develop confidence and control — in short, you will become competent. You won't be tossed around at the whim of the sea, but you'll be able to enjoy yourself in this new environment.

As you gain experience and skill, you will find a far greater range of possibilities than you expected in the beginning when you were stiff and a little clumsy and frightened. This means that you'll not only be able to experiment with the placing of your feet but also with the degree of crouch or knee bend that you find comfortable. When it's most difficult to keep your balance and control, your crouch will be most pronounced. Most surfers bend more at the knees and waist as beginners than they do later on when they have gained more skill.

Arms and Hands

The arms and hands are the most important help in balance throughout a ride. They do for a surfer what the horizontal pole

34

The importance of using arms and hands properly

does for a high-wire performer. The more skilled and stable he is, the less he needs to use the pole, and the best artists often do without it. In the beginning, you'll find your arms in frantic, jerky movements. In time, however, your movements will become less noticeable. You need your arm and hand motions — but less than a lot of beginners think. Some new surfers think that a show of wildly waving arms is impressive to those watching on shore. It isn't. By all means learn to use your arms and hands and legs. If you use them properly — with a minimum amount of movement and effort — you've become captain of your board and not just a passenger hanging on for dear life on a wild ride.

Shuffling the Feet
for Trim Adjustment

The board trim — its angle in the water as seen from the side — is adjusted most of all by shifting the body weight between your front and rear foot. If the nose rides too high, the weight is shifted to the front foot; if too low, to the rear foot.

Picking the
Highest Wave Peak

As the surfer, waiting beyond the breaker line, watches incoming swells, he notes carefully where the highest peaks are formed along the line of each wave. Generally, the conditions of the ocean bottom and the currents will create peaks in waves. Breaking through rarely happens all at once along an entire wave line, especially at beaches that are known for good surfing.

In view of the great stress placed on safety in this book, it might seem rash to choose the highest peaks for takeoff. It might be rash if this were your very first time out on a board. But by now you've gained a certain degree of competence. In surfing as in flying a plane, there is a certain safety in height. A flier whose plane suffers mechanical failure at a high altitude can glide a longer time and has a greater choice of landing spots. The surfer who takes off from a peak has the height and slope of the water ahead to give him greater freedom in his choice of direction. Not

Choosing the highest wave peak

36

only does this give you a more satisfying, exciting ride, but it is safer because you can see any nearby riders or loose boards that may present a real danger.

Pearling

Let's face it — pearling is common with beginners and it's unpleasant. It often makes you look and feel foolish and it can sometimes cause you discomfort, if not outright pain. But there's nothing about pearling to make you ashamed or want to keep it a secret. Even the supersurfers, those who challenge the towering, missile-fast waves of Hawaii and Australia, do it.

If you pearl too often, even as a beginner, it is probably because you haven't bothered to learn enough about judging waves, better timing in takeoff, faster weight-shifting, and better use of turning and angling techniques during the slide down the wave.

1. If you *never* pearl, you're probably playing it too safe.

2. After you've become a fair beginning surfer, you shouldn't pearl more than once or twice in every ten takeoffs.

3. If you become secretive or ashamed of pearling, you're wasting your sensitivity. You don't have to boast about a string of pearls, but you should have patience and a determination to improve.

4. Finally: even in the worst kind of pearl, try not to lose control of your board. If at all possible, don't let it fly wild in the wave, for it can injure you as well as others. Remember, as a surfer you're responsible for the safety of others, just as they are for yours.

Pearling

39

Steering the Surfboard

The basic operation of steering by leaning in the direction of the desired turn was learned in connection with prone or kneeling rides. To turn toward the left, sweep out harder with your right arm while taking no stroke with the left, or possibly even hold your left palm outward against the water as a brake.

Such reverse paddling has a tendency to turn your body rather than your board. To prevent this, you can use your legs and feet to lock the board. Shift the left leg over so that the inside of the foot rests against the rail of the board and the foot drags in the water, toes downward. This will transmit the turning motion to the board and also slow the left side of the board by means of the foot drag. For a right turn do the reverse, lock the right leg against the rail and drag the right foot. But the greater a surfer's paddling power and skill, the less likely he'll need to apply braking action with either his hand or foot.

Steering a surfboard while standing is different, and more difficult, because your only control over the board is now concentrated in two limited areas of contact — where your feet touch the deck.

Actually, only a flat-footed rider has *two* such areas. If your feet are well arched, you really have *four* contact areas: the heels and balls of both feet. Movements of the board are the result of pressure or torque (twisting force) applied through these small contact areas.

We've learned to steer in two different ways:

1. By direct action of the limbs: the arms, as in paddling or back-paddling, or the legs, when one or the other foot is dragged.

2. Steering by leaning or tilting to one side or another, thus making the deeper side slide more slowly through the water than the higher side.

As you gain experience and confidence, you will find that you can steer your board without slipping a hand or foot in the

40

Two methods of turning by tilting

water — with much less risk to your speed and balance. You can do this using three typical turns: the *tilt, tail-down,* and *torque.*

In actual practice, one type of turn may blend into another. But to study them we speak of them as being separate kinds of turns. All have one basic thing in common: they are executed only by the control that you exercise on the board through your feet. And your feet simply provide the contact points for your legs, which transmit the force (downward pressure, twisting motions, and so on) that you start by using the entire body, including your trunk, head, and arms.

Tilt — the rider leans so as to tilt the board in the direction in which his toes point. He leans forward, pressing with the balls of his feet and with his toes. Leaning right forces the right rail

41

Turning tail-down

of the board deeper in the water and the board begins to turn·to the right.

Tail-Down — The rider shifts much of his weight to his rear foot. This makes the tail go low and the nose high. Then the rider uses his front foot to drag the nose of the board around in the direction he wants.

Torque — This is just "more" than the others. The rider leans more, the feet push in opposite directions. The rider's shoulders and arms are swung swiftly in the direction of the turn.

Thus far you've learned the fundamental surfing techniques: paddling, takeoff, balancing, basic turns, and the like. On this foundation you will develop a variety of new techniques.

Keep in mind, however, that to master these basic moves, you'll have to practice and practice long hours. It isn't really

A torque turn

necessary to ride the wave all the way into the beach. More practice, more time on the waves, can be gained by taking many short rides. By doing this you can concentrate on the takeoff and pullout. Practice also helps the new surfer to learn to judge the break and select the best takeoff point. With practice the beginner can master the one or two stroke takeoff, thus saving a lot of energy needed to paddle out for another ride.

Getting Out of Waves

As you master new techniques for fast surfing and steering, you also need to learn new ways to take yourself and board *out of* waves, to end your ride safely and, ideally, even gracefully.

What if, just at the moment you drop into a wave and are

43

about to start your slide down, you realize that the slope before you is too steep to handle?

One way to escape it is the *sternward stall.* If you're standing, you swiftly shuffle back toward the stern until your weight is near the tailblock. As you do this, the nose lifts, the tailblock sinks, and the board is taken out of the wave. Often, dropping to a sitting position on the tail will stall the board even more quickly. As an added measure you can back-paddle as best you can with one or both arms. Such quick action can stop you from a plunge that might cause trouble.

You can also stall with a forward fall. Crouching near the tailblock, the surfer drops forward and catches the front of the board with his two arms as it rears up to him. This way the stall can be quickly changed into a prone paddling position with the surfer ready to turn the board and take it out beyond the surf area again.

A word of caution: don't be too enthusiastic shuffling back. You could go right over the end of your board. Don't ever violate the Great Commandment of surfing: *You shall not lose your board!*

The *leap-off and stall* sounds more derring-do than it really is. It's a simple method of taking the board out of a wave. The standing surfer jumps backward off the side of the board. As he drops, one or both arms are stretched out to catch and cling to the board. For just an instant the board is free. A split second later, the surfer is beside his board, gripping it firmly.

Leaving the Board

You've just been warned to stay with the board at all times. Unfortunately, that's not always possible.

With rare exceptions, the safest way off a board is off the

44

stern. The actual leaving may be by a walk or run to the rear and a dive into the water.

If you go off the rear, the board should be to your front. Then it can't come in from behind and give you a bash on the head. The surfer who has ditched in the water for safety should stay underwater as long as possible holding the following position: head bent forward, chin against the chest, hands laced together at the base of the skull to protect the area from a blow, elbows forward to protect the face. This position doesn't ensure full protection, but it does greatly reduce the risk. Rising to the surface, the surfer should extend an arm above the head to serve as a "feeler."

Even if your board is to your front when you ditch, it can be whipped around and sucked under by surf. Today's light boards can shoot out with great force and then plop back with a shattering smack. This can happen even in comparatively shallow water near shore. So keep a sharp eye out for your board wherever you ditch.

Surf Safety

Swimming, boating, skin diving, water-skiing, and surfing accidents are almost always preventable. The extra person overloading the boat, the novice skin diver with his first scuba, the poor swimmer trying to make it across the lake, and the beginning surfer riding a wipe-out all chance drowning because they lack experience and skill. Safety in *all* water sports boils down to following these basic instructions:

1. Become a strong swimmer.
2. Know your limitations and abilities.
3. Understand the hazards of the sport.
4. Learn the dangers of the particular area in which you surf.
5. Learn and practice rescue skills, first aid, and artificial respiration techniques.
6. Use the "buddy" system while swimming or surfing. A partner provides safety as well as companionship.

Plan Ahead

A few minutes spent wave watching, current guessing, and weather predicting will make all water sports safer. Avoid dangerous situations where violent collisions are possible, where waves can't be ridden safely, and where rocks and currents create hazards you can't escape.

Surfing accidents are caused by collision with another board or rocks, or a blasting wipe-out. Many accidents happen when a board pearls, shoots up in the air, and comes down on the owner or another surfer. This can be prevented with good board control — the skill to cut out of a wave quickly, turn back, stall, and make a successful pullout. These basic skills should be learned as quickly as possible.

A collision

Too many beginners slide a wave with no idea of how to guide their boards or avoid a wipe-out. *Protect yourself at all times:* that's the watchword in surfing. As the sailors on old wooden ships used to say: "One hand for the ship and one for yourself." That means one hand hangs onto the board and the other curls over your head as protection from a skeg zipping past.

The Wipe-Out

Surfers talk endlessly about wipe-outs. They are as much a part of surfing as are the waves. They happen over and over again,

A wipe-out

and how serious they are depends on several things. A wipe-out in deep water with no rocks below isn't as dangerous as a ride over the falls in the shorebreak. The little wipe-outs in shallow water, with other surfers and boards close by, are as big a danger as being smothered by a big wave.

Most beginners know nothing about how to safely handle a wipe-out. Of course, you try to avoid one if at all possible. A spill can mean a long swim, being caught in a rip current, and possibly being hit by your own board.

The simplest way to avoid a wipe-out is to kick out of a wave. Stay alert, anticipate what the wave is going to do, and judge the right time to pull out. It's natural to try and stay in the wave as long as possible, but there's a split second when it's either kick out or get blasted off the board. Most wipe-outs happen because a surfer stays with a wave too long. Don't press your luck. The sea is too strong to challenge.

You can recognize a wipe-out situation, and after a time you will be able to do this almost by instinct. You don't even have to see it; you can feel it through your board. The wave crests suddenly, and a great amount of whiteness will begin to tower over or around you. If you try to ride the wave too close into shore, it will suddenly collapse around you and rush up the beach with you and the board rolling around together. Another kind of wipe-out starts as the wave begins to break in front of you. This is another sure signal that it's time to kick out or take a spill.

If a wipe-out can't be prevented, it can sometimes be controlled. If it's coming and you can't kick out, you can sometimes turn the board toward shore and ride the white water lying prone. The expert rider can cut shoreward, remain standing, and ride the soup in. Beginners will have better luck controlling the board by dropping to their knees and then their stomachs and riding in this way. When you are prone, the weight should be shifted quite far back to keep the nose of the board up and pre-

49

Avoiding a lost board

vent pearling. *Proning in* is a good technique to use because a surfer keeps control of his board, avoids a swim or walk over the rocks, and won't get hit by his own board. Practice riding prone. It's a skill that will often come in handy.

If the wipe-out is sudden and strong, and you know the board will be ripped from your grasp, try to keep away from it. Remember, a board that noses in with great speed is going to come up again, and may fly many feet in the air. If your board has pearled deep enough to come flying up like an underwater missile, you had better dive deep — and the deeper the better. Stay underwater in the protective position mentioned earlier until you're sure the wave and flying board have both passed over.

Wipe-outs in shallow water — where you will be doing most of your first surfing — can be especially dangerous if the bottom is rocky or a coral reef lies below. Try to land with your body flat on the surface of the water, preventing it from diving and smashing on the rocks. After the wipe-out, remember to look around when coming up. You might spot loose boards, surfers coming at you, or another big wave to duck under. Always get a breath of air as soon as you surface — you might have to go under again, and it might be the last breath you will take for some very long seconds.

Rip Currents

Rip currents are caused by massive amounts of seawater piling up in shallow areas near the beach. This water must find a way to flow back and seek its natural level. While doing so it rushes seaward along the easiest path it can find. Strong currents that run out to sea are created this way. Two opposing currents can also create a rip. If currents meet along the shore they will conflict and tend to move seaward until their force is gone.

Rip currents can be recognized by several signs. Since these currents are running along shore or offshore with some speed, they pick up sand and hold it in suspension. The sand gives the water a slightly off-color look. This indicates a rip. A strong rip usually has a triangle of lighter colored water or foam pointing out to sea. Most rips aren't very wide, perhaps twenty yards. Even a strong swimmer will have great trouble moving against one. The best rule is not to fight it — go along with it until it begins to lose force, then circle toward shore out of the rip.

Winds

The great ground swells that roll across the surface of the sea and break on beaches are born of strong winds.

A windstorm may have blown itself out three or four days earlier and from five to ten thousand miles distant from shore. Then, as the great swells arrive, bringing with them this energy born far away, they may cross and mingle with other swells newly whipped up by local winds. The combination of long ground swells and shorter wind swells, in fact, bring about the changes in wave "beats" that surfers call *sets*.

Strong winds in surfing areas can, and often do, bring about drastic and surprising changes. Every surfer should learn to understand what can happen, recognize it when it starts, and deal with it sensibly.

For example, a strong wind blowing from the water to the shore — an *onshore* wind — adds energy to the incoming swells. It makes them peak somewhat sooner and break farther out than they would in a calm. A strong *offshore* wind resists the incoming swells, absorbs some of their strength, and delays their breaking, so that they're closer to shore and over shallower water when they finally break. Lateral winds (blowing from either side) have different effects. A surfer doesn't really know any beach or surfing area until he's seen it under winds of different strengths and directions.

Judging Waves

Judging where, when, and how waves break is an important part of surfing. Being fairly sure how a wave will form, crest, and roll shoreward gives you a good advantage for planning a ride and enjoying it in confidence and safety.

The form of a wave before it becomes a breaker determines whether it can be ridden, how far the ride will go, and the possibilities of a wipe-out. From the beach you can get a fair idea of which way the swell is running and if good shoulders for riding are being formed. A wave that dumps over and crashes along its entire length just can't be ridden — unless it spills gradually and you want to ride white water. *Look for a wave that breaks from one side.* Perhaps the swell of the ocean is low and only one or two waves of a set are good for riding. If you recognize these in advance, you'll have a ride. Look for swells that have one side lower than the other . . . the lower portions break later.

Suppose a wave looks good and the surfer decides to try for it, and makes his start and turn. As he rides he'll be able to notice if the wave is peaking up in front to a degree that it will spill over and break in front of him. If the wave is about to break, it is time either to pull out or ride shoreward in a prone position. Most wipe-outs happen because the surfer stays in the wave too long and doesn't pull out in time. Each wave is different — and you must make a decision based on a quick look at the wave. Watch carefully and learn the signs of the surf.

Some Other Hazards of Surfing

Sharks: You probably will never see a shark, but sharks are the greatest danger to surfers. They are present around all beaches of the world and they may venture close to shore.

If you cut yourself — even in shallow water — get into shore fast. Blood attracts sharks far beyond their ability to see. The

53

Check for wave direction

shark's sense of smell is incredible. Don't take food out to munch while lazing on a board, waiting for a wave.

Most shark attacks occur off Australia, but they are a danger even in American coastal waters, especially in warm weather when you'll be doing your surfing. Although sharks rarely venture into shallow water, it's best to play it safe — if you sight a dorsal fin, or hear someone shout the warning, get out of the water fast and with as little panic as possible.

Sea urchins: Usually found in tropical waters, sea urchins look like fat purple or black pincushions with very long needles sticking point upward. They usually collect in rocky areas. Stay away from them.

Coral: This is also found in tropical waters. The sharp surfaces of coral can give you a deep laceration that allows micro-

54

A wet suit

scopic bacteria to enter the body. Coral poisoning is a serious infection, and cuts from coral should be treated immediately.

Cold water and fatigue: When the water temperature drops and the wind is blowing, the surfer sitting on a wet board, with wet hair, skin, and trunks loses body heat very rapidly. Muscles become stiff and tense, the body starts shaking, and the hands and feet grow numb. Fine control of the board — so necessary for safety — is no longer possible. You're no hero if you stay in the water when you're shivering and tired; you're just being foolhardy.

Either avoid cold water or get a *wet suit* surfing shirt. They

55

are comparatively inexpensive and are worth the cost for the extra comfort and safety they provide.

Surfing Rules
of the Road

Surf at your own level of skill. Take a wave only if your skill can handle it.

Allow the expert the advantage if several persons are taking off on the same wave. He knows how to avoid collisions.

Avoid riding toward surfers paddling out. The rider on a wave has more control than a paddler. Always anticipate having to cut and turn away from others. If you can only avoid a collision by losing a wave — lose it — there will be other waves.

Avoid areas where there are swimmers or bathers. Young children don't realize the danger of a surfboard rushing into shore. They'll often run to grab it. Check the surfing regulations with the lifeguard at your local beach.

Don't force another surfer to drop out of a wave. If the wave is crowded, the man in front farthest from the break should avoid cutting back into other surfers.

Don't take off directly in front of another rider. A surfer sliding a fast wall might not be able to cut back and then let the person taking off get started and turn. Any collision course should be avoided.

Paddlers going out should work their way around the direct route of incoming surfers. Paddlers also have a responsibility to avoid collisions. You can be facing fifteen riders coming in. If one stops to avoid you, the rest will usually jam up and spill or collide like a chain accident on a highway.

Keep your board in good repair. Loose flaps of fiberglass, rough rails, and jagged edges on the skeg can cut and tear the skin.

Avoid surfers paddling out

Don't lose control of your board. We've discussed this number one safety rule a great deal. If your board is kept thoroughly waxed, the chances of slipping are less and control is better. It's just good sense not to lose your board.

And last: *Surf with a heads-up attitude.* Be aware of what's happening to the wave you're riding. Know where other surfers are, and use your eyes to tell you of hazards and anything else that will affect your safety on the ride in and paddle out.

57

Avoid taking off in front of another rider

Modern surfing is youth itself . . . sun, sea, and air . . . a challenge to meet . . . new skills to learn. The sea is old — but you are young, getting a sense of your body, feeling new surges of energy. We involve ourselves in sports to define what we are, what we can do, what we will be. And there is no better way in the world to give you the knowledge of yourself, the confidence for living, than to meet the great grizzled oceans and learn to live in them.

GOOD LUCK — AND GOOD SURFING!

58

Glossary

Angling — Sliding across the face of a wave, either right or left.

Backwash — The rush of water down the slope of a beach after a wave has run up the beach.

Bailing Out — A planned escape from a surfboard just before a wipe-out.

Belly Board—A short surfboard propelled mainly by kicking.

Channel — A spot of deep water where the surf doesn't usually form; a good place to paddle out.

Choppy — A ruffled water surface caused by winds.

Climbing — Angling up the face of the wave toward the crest.

Crest — The top portion of a wave. When a wave is cresting, it is just beginning to spill over and break.

Curl — The portion of the wave that is spilling over and breaking.

Cut Out — To pull out of the wave, like kicking out.

Deck — The top surface of the surfboard.

Drop — The first downward slide made during the start.

Face — The unbroken front of the wave.

Fiberglass — Material made from glass that is used to make surfboards.

Grabbing the Rail — A pullout technique accomplished by grabbing the rail on the side away from the wave and pulling the board into the wave to keep the board from being washed away.

Inshore — The place in the water just off the beach and inside the break.

Kick Out — Pushing down on the tail of the board to lift and turn the nose over the top of the wave.

Left Slide — Riding a wave to the surfer's left.

Outside — The area beyond where the surf is breaking. Also the yell or warning that a wave is coming.

Over the Falls — Being driven down with the breaking part of the wave, toward the bottom, with force.

Paddleboard — A hollow wooden (or very light foam) elongated surfboard used primarily for travel across the water. Most paddleboards are awkward in the surf.

Peak — The highest part of the wave.

Pearl — A surfboard "pearls" when the nose drops enough to dig in and slow or stop the board.

Pullout — Ending the ride and getting off the wave by steering the board over, or through, the face of the wave.

Rails — The rounded edges of the surfboard.

Rip Current — A volume of water moving seaward or parallel to shore caused by massive amounts of water piling up along shore and then moving out to seek its natural level.

Set — A group of waves.

Shorebreak — Waves that break on the shore with a lot of energy. Surf is not breaking well for riding.

Shoulder — The unbroken portion of the wave next to the white water.

Shuffle — A movement toward the nose (or rear) of the board done by moving one foot after another and not crossing the feet.

Skeg — The fin at the tail of the board.

Sliding — Riding down the wave after catching it.

Soup — The foamy part of the broken wave, the white water.

Stall — Slowing the board after it outraces the wave, so that the break can catch up with the surfer.

Swells — Unbroken waves moving in groups of similar height and period.

Tail — The stern or rear end of the surfboard.

Takeoff — The start of a ride.

Trim — To steer the board so it planes most efficiently across the face of a wave. A board in trim should be moving at maximum speed and stability.

Trough — The lowest part between the crests of two successive waves.

Undertow — No such thing exists.

Walking the Nose — Moving forward on the board toward the front or nose.

Wall — The face of a wave, usually steep and unbroken.

Wet Suit — A neoprene rubber suit used by surfers and skin-divers to keep warm. A wet suit allows water to enter between the rubber and the skin. The water is then trapped and warmed by the body.

White Water — The white, bubbly, foamy part of a broken wave. It is also called soup.

Wipe-Out — Falling or being knocked down, blown, or pushed off a board by a collapsing wave.

Bibliography

Connor, James III. *Surfing Summer*. New York: William R. Scott, 1969.

A novel about two teenagers and the summer they learned to surf.

Cook, Joseph J. & Romeika, William J. *Better Surfing for Boys*. New York: Dodd, Mead, 1967.

A short, basic book on the fundamentals of surfing. Photos.

Dixon, Peter L. *The Complete Book of Surfing*. New York: Coward-McCann, 1969.

A well-written, knowledgeable, comprehensive guide to surfing. Over 100 photos.

Dixon, Peter L., ed. *Men and Waves*. New York: Coward-McCann, 1966.

An anthology of the history, science, lore, adventure, fiction and facts of surfing. Excellent photos.

Finney, Ben R. & Houston, James D. *Surfing: The Sport of Hawaiian Kings*. Rutland, Vt.: Charles E. Tuttle Co., 1966.

Explores surfing's colorful history with island legends. Many photos, early prints, and engravings.

Gardner, Robert L. *The Art of Body Surfing*. Philadelphia: Chilton, 1972.

An excellent preparation for board-surfing. Photos.

Halacy, D. S. Jr. *Surfer*. New York: Macmillan, 1965.

An action-packed novel about a high school student and the Neptunes, the best surfing club on the west coast.

Klein, Arthur H. *Surfing*. Philadelphia: J. B. Lippincott Co., 1965.

> An authoritative, practical guide to every aspect of surfing. Many photos and diagrams.

Kuhns, Grant. *On Surfing*. Rutland, Vt.: Charles E. Tuttle Co., 1963.

> A step-by-step instructional book on the techniques and mystiques of surfing. Maps, diagrams, photos, and illustrations.

Patterson, O. B. *Surf-Riding*. Rutland, Vt.: Charles E. Tuttle Co., 1960.

> Part instruction, part travel guide to surfing areas around the world. Photos and diagrams.

Pollard, Jack, ed. *The Surfrider*. New York: Taplinger Publishing Co., 1968.

> A complete guide to surfing written by seventeen experts, from selection of a board to the fine points of competitive surfing. 133 photos.

Index

Torque, 42
Training, 5-6
Treading water, 5
Trim, 36, 61
Trough, 61
Turning, 20-21, 28
Turning turtle, 24
Turns, 41-42

Undertows, 10-11, 61
U.S. Surfing Association, 8

Walking the nose, 61
Walls, of wave, 61

Waves:
    for body surfing, 7
    broken, 25-28
    catching (riding), 7, 28-31
    getting out of, 43-44
    highest peak, 36
    judging, 53
    sets, 15, 60
Waxing, 14-15
Weight shifting, 32, 36
Wet suits, 55, 61
White water, 61
Winds, 9, 52
Wipe-outs, 47-51, 61